Encounters with Angels

Dan Lindholm

Encounters with Angels

Floris Books

Translated by Donald Maclean

First published in German as *Vom Engel berührt*
by Verlag Freies Geistesleben, Stuttgart, 1989.
Published in Norwegian as *Kjenner du din engel*
by Antropos Forlag, Oslo, 1989.
English version first published in 1991 by Floris Books.
Reprinted in 1993.

© 1989 Verlag Freies Geistesleben.
This translation © 1991 Floris Books.

British Library CIP data available.

ISBN 0–86315–137–X

Printed in Great Britain
by Bookcraft Ltd.

Contents

1 Can we believe in angels?

We may sometimes pause for a moment and wonder whether angels really exist, but almost at once the demands of life claim our attention and the question slips from our mind. For my youngest brother, though, there was never any doubt. Looking back on his early childhood, he recounts:

"I remember clearly my little bed, for on one of the bars was attached my most precious possession — the picture of an angel! From above white clouds he came sweeping down to me. Every night I looked forward to finishing my evening prayer and the grown–ups' good night. Then I lay there by myself but I was not alone. From the picture of the angel there shone a gentle light filling me with happiness and trust. A being detached itself as it were from that simple picture, grew and came near me ... After all these years, I can still say today how true that was."

But what of those of us who are no longer children? Can we really believe in angels, believe that real spiritual beings exist and are present? Perhaps we have our doubts. Let us however listen to those who have had experiences in this area. The present writer simply listened to others and their accounts, and what he put down on paper is no more than what he has been told or what he has read about. He has added nothing of his own. At the end, the reader is free to form his own opinion. Of course the stories which follow will have a personal colouring and so may be seen as subjective experiences, perhaps not always presented with cool detachment, but this in no way diminishes their intrinsic truth.

And now to begin with what I myself can vouch for.

We children received from our dear mother the good advice that we should not run to God our Father with every little bump or bruise.

"He's got more to do than just blow on our small chilblains," said she. "Show him rather that you can take a knock! Furthermore he has given you an angel as a companion through life. If the going gets bad, you can pray to your angel for help! For he is ready to help you. Remember the story of the companion."

And she told the following story:

Now, there was once a boy who dreamed about a wonderfully beautiful princess. And when he awoke, he felt that he simply could not go on living unless he found the princess. The little that he owned he sold for money and set off. Then he came to a church and in front of the church door stood a man frozen inside a block of ice. When the congregation came out of the church, they spat upon the man in the block of ice. The boy asked the priest why they did that.

"Because he was a great sinner," answered the priest.

Then the boy wanted to know what kind of sin the man had committed.

"He mixed water in his wine," answered the priest.

The boy thought that there were greater sins than that, and he asked whether the man would be allowed to be buried in Christian ground seeing that he had paid the penalty for his sin with his life.

"That costs money," replied the priest, "and who do you think will pay for the burial?"

"Well," said the boy, "if you will bury the man in Christian ground, I will pay the cost."

This offer was accepted and the man was buried. The boy then continued on his travels until he came to a country where all the roads went straight ahead without any turnings. As he was going along, someone came up behind him, tapped him on the shoulder and asked him if he needed a servant. But now the boy had no more money with which to pay a servant. The stranger said:

"Do not worry about the wages. I know that you require a companion; we shall share whatever comes our way."

The picture of the companion frozen into the block of ice has never left me. Without his help, the boy would never have found the princess that he had dreamed of. The companion in the block of ice became an image of the angel who sits frozen fast in our cold material-istic intellect — longing for the heart's warmth that can set him free.

It was not long till I needed help from my own companion. I was seven years old at the time, and it was Christmastime. Under the glittering tree there lay a present for me: a box of coloured crayons. The box fitted beautifully into the pocket of my home-made trousers. This pocket was sewn on to the seat of my trousers, which had not pleased me so much when I was given the trousers, but now I was delighted as the box peeped out and everyone could admire it in all its glory when I twirled round.

Every evening was a festival for us children, for

then father would draw pictures or tell stories. They were long stories and always exciting. Once when he was right in the middle he suddenly asked:

"Lend me your crayons, little fellow!"

I felt in my back-pocket. Oh help, it was empty! Whatever I answered I cannot remember now. But I am sure I must have gone red with embarrassment.

The next day I searched high and low, inside and outside. Where could the crayons have gone? As evening approached, I grew more and more uneasy, for I knew that I should be asked later about the crayons. And sure enough:

"Have you found the box?"

I tried to avoid answering. Father looked up briefly from his drawing:

"See that you find it."

Once I was in bed that night, I prayed with all my soul to my angel. I was as unhappy as only a child can be, and when I woke up the next morning I prayed again that he would let me find my coloured crayons.

Then there happened what I can only describe with difficulty. I began to walk first down the stairs, then through the passage and out into the courtyard, and a little bit over the road. On both sides there were fields clear of snow with withered frosty grass. I turned off a few steps from the road, and there beside a clump lay the box. Even today after so many years I can see it in front of me. It seemed a miracle for I could have sworn that I had not gone into that field before.

Have I been faithful to my companion? I would rather answer the reverse question. He has been faithful to a soul often perplexed and bewildered. In the first place we were all growing up and eager to take part in the dance of life as it were. Then there was not much talk of angels. But as time went on, first one then another left the dance–floor; and in the end so did I. Destiny was calling.

Late one evening I lay on my bed, nursing a deep grievance, for I felt I had been wronged by her who meant more to me than any other person. I battled with my sullen resentment, saying to myself that she could not possibly know how deeply her little remark had wounded me. I have never experienced such a violent conflict between sternly controlled thought and tempestuous emotions. With all my strength, I tried to take my feelings in hand. And with the help of higher thoughts I succeeded in calming my soul.

Then quite unexpectedly I experienced something which never happened to me before nor since. The power of thought became so compulsive and powerful that I was sure that it would show itself in its full reality, and make manifest its intrinsic nature.

"Think of your angel," said I to myself, "and he will reveal himself to you!"

At that same moment my eyes were filled with a blinding light. A being of tremendous intensity was in the light, with such a mighty presence that I felt my little self overcome with a bewildering fear.

"No, no! " I cried, "I cannot bear it!"

The light vanished and so did my fear. As a reaction, I was filled with an unbounded feeling of shame at my own weakness. Once more I tried and the whole thing happened again: the blinding light, the fear and the feeling of shame.

Later I got to know that, in exactly the same way, other people have experienced the encounter with a higher spiritual being. An almost unconquerable fear of the spirit's might sits deeply imbedded in our souls, and even the fear of ghosts lurks at the edges of our consciousness. Undoubtedly there is a reason for this fear: remember how in the Scriptures every time an angel appears we hear the greeting: "Fear not!"

Though this kind of encounter with higher powers is overwhelming, we should not forget either the sudden little flashes of inspiration when we are blessed with a new idea or the solution of a problem. Where do they come from, these small shooting-stars which now and again light up in our inmost being, often in decisive moments? This is the question which poses itself when we examine our thought-life attentively.

That all sorts of things come up through the cracks in the floor of our consciousness is sure enough. Official science speaks about the subconscious, that "open sesame" of modern psychology. But seldom are we told how we should imagine this subconscious — rather like a spiritual bucket into which all the repressed and forgotten débris of life is dumped? And out of this offal come our good ideas and genial inspiration? There seems to be something missing in the picture. No one would dream of explaining a plant merely by pointing to the earth in which it grows. We know that the sun's life-giving light and warmth are at least just as necessary. Can it not be the same with the human soul? Should we not rather look for a higher awareness, a *super*conscious state of soul, a light-space, a spiritual vault above our life on earth, filled with beings who watch over our human ways and works?

These reflections stem from a personal experience.

On one of those days between winter and spring, I stepped out of a shop. The street was almost empty. Without thinking very much I went a little way but suddenly I stopped for a moment. Perhaps I was looking to see if I could cross the street, I cannot say for certain. But at that moment a large heavy sheet of ice slid from the roof of a five-storeyed building and crashed down violently on to the pavement less than two paces ahead of me!

"That was a near thing!" exclaimed a startled man coming towards me.

It is quite certain that if I had not stopped for a moment "by chance," I should not be sitting here now writing about it.

Many will say it was "pure chance" that I escaped, but for such people then all life must appear as "pure chance." Was it "by chance" that I was born, is it "by chance" that I exist? In this kind of thinking, the succession of chances is never-ending, and life remains a dark mystery unlit by knowledge of the spirit. But for me it is otherwise.

Certainly at first I felt quite unconcerned about "my lucky escape." It was as if the falling ice had nothing to do with me. Only when I came to think about it afterwards did it dawn on me that perhaps my angel had spoken, and that I ought to find the right response, for my life had been given to me afresh.

Which is to say that, purely abstractly one can imagine anything. But a more realistic train of thought, a thinking which holds fast to the realities in our existence cannot lay chance as the foundation for our life on earth. If it does it removes its own precondition, namely the fact of our own existence.

Each human life is a mystery which each of us

lives. Under the progress of materialism, life itself becomes more and more a dark mystery. But it does not need to remain dark forever. The mystery will remain; and a new science of the spirit will be able gradually to illumine it.

2 A child's dream

For us children it was a treat when old Andreas
Austlid came into our house. His long hair and his
silver–grey beard made him look like of an Old
Testament prophet. His face was full of a mild earnestness, and his kindly eyes seemed to look far into
another world.

Andreas Austlid had been a school teacher and
could tell stories like no one else; about remarkable
events of long ago, about Visknut the seer, about the
"Skottetog" (the expedition from Scotland in the
seventeenth century which ended disastrously in the
battle of Kringom) and other sagas and stories. We
listened eagerly and always asked for more. Also we
loved to hear about his own childhood on his father's
farm.

And here is the story of his angel as he told it
himself:

*I was about four years old or thereabouts and one day
I was playing in the garden. I happened to see an
animal up in a birch–tree. I thought it must be a
kitten, but it was only a squirrel. It hopped away
down the hill and I wanted to catch it, but the little
creature sprang away.*

*The game went on in this way for a while till it ran
away behind a stone. By then I had wandered quite a
long way and I did not know any more where I was.
I started to cry and call for my mother but no one*

heard me. In the end I grew so tired that I lay down in a hollow in the grass and fell asleep.

While I was sleeping, I dreamed that an angel came to me. He was dressed in white and had a golden belt round his body, and it was so bright that it shone from him. He unfastened his belt, gave me one end and told me that if I held tight I should go with him to heaven. But I did not dare catch hold of the belt because it was so beautiful, and I thought that my hands were not clean. The angel said that he would look after me.

I woke up. I saw that there was an adder looking at me. But then my father came striding along and the snake wriggled away and disappeared into a bush. My father lifted me up and then my mother came running up. They were overjoyed because they had been out for many hours looking for me.

3 Ibsen's dream

How different from Andreas Austlid's was Henrik Ibsen's dream of the angel. His classmate from school in Skien, later to become Deacon Boye Ording, narrates how the pupils had been given the title "A Dream" for their essay–writing.

"I shall never forget how quiet we were when Ibsen read out his essay," says Ording. "How strongly it affected my mind." He retells Ibsen's dream from memory:

While on a long walk in the country, we were over–taken by darkness. Weary and lost we lay down to rest like Jacob of old with a stone for a pillow. My companions were soon asleep but for a long time I could not sleep, though finally exhaustion overcame me. In a dream I saw an angel standing over me, saying:

"Arise and follow me."

"Whither wilt thou lead me in this darkness," I asked.

"Come," he replied, "I shall show thee a sight: man's life in its reality and truth!"

In fear I followed him. Down tremendous stairs he led me until the mountains leaned over us in mighty arches. Down below there stood a huge city of death with all the fearful signs of mortality and transience, a whole world lay as a corpse, sunk together under the power of death, a pale, withered, worn–out glory. Over everything there shone a dim light, like the gloomy reflection cast over a graveyard by the whitewashed church walls and a white painted cross. In this eerie light, endless rows of bleached bones filled the dark space. This sight cast an icy terror over me as I stood by the angel's side.

"Here thou seest, all is passing away," said he.

Then there came a rushing noise like the first blast of a tempest, a thousandfold groaning sigh which grew to a howling storm as the dead moved and stretched their arms out towards me ... In a fright I awoke, wet with the night's cold dew.

Many years later, when Ibsen had long since become a world-famous poet, he was reminded of this dream and confirmed that it had happened. He recalled that the teacher refused to believe that Ibsen himself had written the essay, and this led to a long misunderstanding between teacher and pupil.

Ording adds delicately that it had often seemed to him since then that in this dream was something prophetic, a presage of the whole of Ibsen's later life as a poet, that what he experienced in his boyhood dream became the recurrent underlying theme in his poetry.

4 Henrik Wergeland

Where sweet intoxication streams
From birch in glen so deep,
Beneath an angel's shield my dreams
With bliss have filled my sleep.

If we were to single out a Norwegian poet inspired by angels, then above all others it would have to be Henrik Wergeland.

It would take far too long to trace all the angels in his innumerable poems and in the great work of his youth, *Creatures, Man and Messiah.* Here we must content ourselves with a story from *Hazelnuts,* the memoirs written on his last sickbed.

Before he became the parish priest in Eidsvoll, Wergeland grew up in Kristiansand. From his earliest childhood there, somewhere around the age of three or four, he recalls going on a little walk with his parents in the English Park, as it was called. For a moment he found himself alone, probably because his parents had stopped to chat with some acquaintance or other. To continue the story in his own words:

Suddenly I found myself alone in front of a cliff–face where huge crystals shone in all colours. It was as if the trees had been moved to one side so as to show me the sight. At first I was frightened, but then I became absorbed in contemplating all this splendour. And even today this wonderful vision appears before

*me in all its first freshness. Indeed every time I look
into a glass prism or into a kaleidoscope, I am
reminded of it.*

No grown-up would believe what he told them; the
only believer was a half-witted little girl. Some years
later Wergeland tried to find the place again. But it
transpired that there was no cliff-face at all in the
English Park.

And what should we believe? In this imaginative
vision of the child, were these the jewels which the
man was to give us in his poetry? And was it perhaps
his angel that bent the trees aside to show him the
vision?

5 The woodcut in the psalm-book

How different from Wergeland's childhood experience
was that of Viktor Rydberg, the famous Swedish poet
and mythologist. When he was seven or eight years
old, he lost his mother and this cast a shadow over his
otherwise happy childhood.

In a poem — in any other form it might not have
been possible — he describes how on one sunny
Sunday he was on the way to church in his home
town of Jönköping. It was springtime and there were
flowers everywhere. The church-bells filled the air
with their mighty sound; young and old alike, dressed
in their best, were gathering for the service in the
town's venerable house of God.

According to ancient custom each one went to his
usual place, and the boy Rydberg went too with his
psalm-book in his hand. The organ played a solemn
prelude, and the congregation began to sing a psalm.
Rydberg opened his psalm-book to sing with them.
There his eye fell upon a woodcut illustration in the
book: King David with his harp in his hand singing
praises to the Lord — surrounded by Zion's heights in
the background — "a wonderful production in the
style of old Lundström." Rydberg then tells us:

*But what glorious beauty I beheld there, what heav-
enly colours! From the strings of the harp which
David was plucking, sparks flew out and became
resonant notes. Already I seemed to hear his voice
and the words of his song:*

21

> *My redeemèd soul shall some time*
> *On Salem's mountains dwell*
> *Where angels' harps are sounding.*

Suddenly I heard a flock of larks singing in jubilation. They took me with them into that blessed region of the azure–blue ether. It was as if my soul had been given a pair of wings and I flew up over the landscape of the holy land, while the earth vanished away as I approached the blessed city of Salem with its towers and minarets.

All the saints swept forward, coming from every corner — I can see them still today — and lo! there was beckoning to me a beloved and glorious figure, my mother who had died, she who had been every-thing to me! I flew to her to rest in her bosom and to cast off my lark's coat of feathers in her lap ...

But oh! now the psalm came to an end. The notes of the organ died away and the thread of my day-dream was broken. Once again I was sitting on the wooden pew. The church seemed cold and empty to me. But still I thought I could feel the nearness of the loved soul who for a moment had shown herself so warm and alive to me.

But he still seemed to feel her invisible presence, his mother's soul who for a moment had shown herself so warm and alive for him.

> *I thought of her*
> *As I sat there*
> *And knew that we two*
> *Were one.*

6 He heard his name

Only rarely, we are told, do the angels reveal themselves to the senses. Sometimes however their reflection is beheld in dreams, or if the mind is released for
a moment from the physical world it can apprehend
the presence of an angel.

Here then is an story told by Johannes Bye, a priest
whose calm clear eyes showed that never an untrue
word passed his lips. In his younger days, Johannes
Bye was sent to Liene in Nord–Trøndelag, an ex-
tended but thinly populated parish. He tells his own
story:

*One winter's day in 1921 I had been visiting the sick
and was on my way home over the mountains between
Sørli and Nordli, the two valleys in which the congregation was divided. I was on skis; in winter it was
hardly possible to travel otherwise. Going up I had
the company of the postman for a bit. He was driving
a horse and sledge and I remember that the horse had
to wear snow–shoes in order to travel over the deep
snow. As we came up on to the uplands, we parted.
The going was good and I thought it would be too
slow keeping company with the horse. The weather
was not bad, but visibility could have been better. The
cloud cover was low over the wide expanse of snow
and gave a diffuse light so that the horizon vanished
in a single white on white, something which one can
often experience up in the mountains. The snow had
been drifting and not much of the track was visible.*

23

But I thought I knew the way well enough, and there was no mistaking the direction. So I set off downhill towards Lake Limingen.

Not a breath of wind stirred, no life was to be seen. There was no other sound but that of the skis and the sticks in the snow. Soon the ground began to slope away down evenly towards Nordli. Suddenly I heard someone call my name: "Johannes Bye!" I stopped and listened. Nothing to be seen. On all sides the country was deserted and empty. It must have been my imagination, I thought, and a trick of hearing. I pushed the stick into the snow to set off again down-hill. But I had hardly gone one or two ski-lengths before I heard my name again quite clearly: "Johannes Bye!" What in all the world had happened to the postman now? I looked back, but no, it could not possibly be him, I had left him out of sight a long time ago. It must have been a hallucination of some kind. I stuck my sticks in once more, for now the ground sloped away nicely. Then I heard for the third time loud and clear that someone called my name. Now there was no doubt: it must be the postman needing help. I turned round and followed my ski-tracks back perhaps for ten minutes or so. And there came the horse and postman driving along happily.

Half unconcerned, I asked:

"Did you call to me?"

No, he had not called, why should he? I said no more, but thought it best to stay in his company.

We followed my ski tracks to the point where I had first heard my name called. There the postman turned sharply away from my tracks and saw that they went on straight ahead. He stopped his horse and pointed.

"Are those your tracks?" he asked. Yes, indeed, I could not deny that. He got up off the sledge.

"Come with me, priest, now you will see a strange thing," he said and followed my tracks. I began to suspect something awful and my heart began to beat hard in my breast. After a few ski–lengths we stood at the edge of a cornice of snow over a precipice more than a hundred feet deep. The white snow merged completely with the white far below so that it was impossible to see the abyss except right at the edge.

Johannes Bye refrains from further comment, which says much for his calm testimony. He must have been in no doubt how easily we can interpret the event so that it fits in with what we want to believe.

7 An Easter greeting

In the First World War, young Johannes Hemleben
was sent to the Eastern Front. At that time there was
no radio contact between army units and, as Hemleben
was a good horseman he was used as a despatch rider.
Later he was to become one of the founders and a
priest of the Christian Community.

On one occasion when we came to talk about
angels — what they are and what they are like, what
tasks they may have, and what help they can give —
he told me of a war-time experience.

*Our troops had advanced into Russian territory. One
of my companions and myself were assigned to
officers who were sent to reconnoitre the enemy
terrain. For the Russians it was Easter, their festival
does not always coincide with ours, for at that time
their Church used a different calendar from ours.
Easter was and in part still is a holy and joyous time
for the Russian people. It was the custom on Easter
morning for people to greet each other with "Christ
is risen!" to which the answer was always, "Verily he
is risen!"*

*But for us the war went on without taking Easter
into account. We had come forward along some
side-roads to a bridge over a fairly broad stream.
There we dismounted and my companion and I were
told to hold the horses for the two officers who
wished to climb onto higher ground from where they*

could spy out the country with their telescopes. We were told not to leave the end of the bridge, but to wait until they returned. Each of us had to hold two horses.

Well, there we stood. A little way below us stood a peasant's house, and just then out came two women who appeared to be mother and daughter. They were carrying Easter eggs in a basket. They waved to us and beckoned to us to come down to them and get some eggs. We could not understand their language but it was not difficult to understand what they meant.

Actually it was forbidden for us soldiers to have any contact with the inhabitants in enemy territory, because of the risk of being enticed into an ambush. But that seemed unthinkable in this case. Also the temptation was too great, so we led the horses down with us to the farmyard where we were offered lovely eggs – a rare treat for front–line soldiers.

Suddenly there came a whine followed by a mighty explosion. We ducked to save ourselves from earth and stone splinters. A heavy–calibre shell had struck exactly the spot where we had been standing with our horses at the end of the bridge. A huge crater now gaped to the sky.

What we felt is not easy to say. But we were certainly shaken. And what can those two good women have felt? They had simply brought an Easter greeting to two enemy soldiers.

For us it was a sign. Perhaps many will say that blind chance saved our lives. It may seem like that from one point of view; but the reality of life is never one–sided. If you actually experience such a thing yourself, you see it differently.

So concluded Hemleben.

When we ponder on such events, we begin to have some insight into the workings of higher powers: how they can bring about an interaction between human souls, souls who had never met before.

8 On an angel's errand

More often than we think, we are prompted by an inexplicable urge to do something unaccustomed — perhaps merely to take a different route from usual, or to go and visit someone who was not especially on our mind. Only afterwards does the thought come to us: on whose errand did we actually go?

Young Eva Schickler tells of such an experience:

I was eighteen at the time and wanting to be regarded more as a young lady than as a pupil in the final year. We lived a little way out of Hamburg, and one grey November day I was sitting as usual in the train of the suburban railway on my way home from school. I had a window-seat and was looking out, tired and dreamy, across the countryside as it rushed past.

Suddenly I was pulled back from my day-dreams. Filled with a strange unease, I looked out of the window as the train was rushing along. Had something gone wrong there in the woods? Nothing could be seen, only the familiar slope up from the track and the thick bushes with the woods behind.

The train stopped and I got out. My bus was waiting. I stood still for a moment, and the unease would not let go of me.

"No," I argued with myself, "you are imagining things!"

I tore myself away and ran over to the bus to catch it. But just as I was setting my foot on the step, I turned round and looked towards the woods.

Something seemed to pull me towards them; I could not help myself, and started running back along the path beside the railway line.

Fairly out of breath I stood there. There was nothing unusual to be seen, only the thick under-growth and the tall fir trunks behind. Now I began to doubt myself, wondering whether my agitation was not the result of fantasy. But my unease still would not leave me. I climbed up the bank and went a little way into the woods. Then, shocked, I stood still, at first not believing my eyes: in a dip was a marsh with a pool, and in the middle of the pool lay a woman sunk nearly up to her armpits. She looked at me with a fixed despairing look. Her ashen grey face was smeared with dirt, her hair full of slime. A ghastly sight! She never said a word. Only her eyes were hypnotically fixed on me.

"Wait a moment," I called.

I ripped off my pullover and threw it to her hoping that it might warm her a bit, which of course it could not do. Then I waded out a bit, but soon noticed that I too would sink in.

"Just keep calm, I'll go and get help," I called to her.

I made my way back to the path and fortunately at that moment along came a young man who came immediately to the rescue. With great exertion we managed to get the woman out of the bog. That took us nearly half an hour. She was naked and blue with cold. Her clothes lay neatly piled in a heap. We wrapped her up in what we could spare of our cloth-ing and I sat with her while the young man went to fetch an ambulance. She showed scarcely any reaction to our efforts, she was too exhausted. But when I explained to her that the ambulance was coming, she smiled weakly. I became quite warm with joy and eagerly rubbed her arms and feet. Poor thing, she was almost dead with cold.

Then the ambulance came, and now everything happened quickly. I said goodbye to the helpful young man, took my wet cloak over my arm and walked home. It was cold and my knees were shaking under me. But I was happy in a way that I had hardly ever been before.

The next day we heard that the woman had been missing for two days from an old people's home. She had tried to take her own life. No one could say how long she had been lying in the marsh. Fortunately there had been a flagstone at the bottom and that had prevented her from sinking right in.

Some days later I visited her. She was sitting in a comfortable chair and beamed with contentment. She pressed to her breast the flowers which I brought her. That was the only time I saw her. A month later she died peacefully in her sleep.

Later I often asked myself what had moved me to go all that way back and to climb up the embankment. For as I was able to verify later the marsh could not be seen from the train.

9 Lost in the forest

About the turn of the century, Karl Sjöblom was a
teacher in Northern Bohuslän in Sweden, hard up
against the Norwegian frontier. One day he was
travelling along a path in the woods. It was snowing
and snowing, endlessly. Silently the snowflakes laid a
thick white carpet over the frozen lakes, woods and
moors. Not a breath of wind stirred the pine trees, but
the weight of the snow bent the young birches so that
they formed arches over the path.

He tells the story in his own words:

*It was so remarkably still, as if a mysterious voice
wanted to whisper something to me. There is a rather
strange feeling when you are so very alone in the
endless forest, especially deep in winter.*

*Thicker and thicker the snow was falling. But there
— what was that now? Fresh footprints right across
the path here in the wilderness? Not the prints of an
animal, but human prints. What could that mean? For
there were few people in those huge forests. Twenty,
thirty paces further — there the tracks came back and
followed the path for a bit. But then they led off
again, and now I saw that those were the fresh tracks,
not yet covered over with snow, of a child. I was
shocked — a child, with night coming on, here in the
vast expanse of the forest!*

*It was clear enough that some poor child had got
lost. By God's blessing I had my lantern, which I lit
to follow the tracks. I knew there were no dwellings*

for miles around. Now every minute would count. I prayed God to save both the child and me. The ground was difficult, that I knew. And it was getting darker and darker. But with the lantern, the tracks were easily visible. The question was: how long would the oil in my lantern last? I would have to keep the flame as low as possible. Again and again I shouted, but I got no other answer than the night's silent darkness. I had to admit that it was eerie, as if the forest's unseen spirits were being disturbed.

It is incredible how someone who is lost can wander about in the maze of the forest. The tracks went round an outcrop of rock and over a frozen bog. In one place the snow was pressed down, apparently the child had fallen or lain down, had probably cried and called out for its mother and father. On and on wound the tracks. In the darkness the child had not noticed the edge of a steep slope. The tracks slid down. I bent over and called. Deep silence. Carefully I tried to climb down, but I missed my foothold and slithered down as well. The snow had covered all the bumps so that I escaped all harm and soon found the tracks again at the bottom.

In this way nearly two hours passed. Now it had stopped snowing, and the moon shone out from behind the clouds just as there was only a tiny little flame left in the lamp. And there in front of me lay a dark bundle in the snow. Completely exhausted the child, a little girl, had fallen down. In the last rays of the lamp I glimpsed the line of tears down her cheeks. When I lifted her up she sighed deeply and sobbed half aloud: "Mama, mama!"

She fell asleep again at once. Poor tiny thing! Her sleep would have been a sleep unto death if providence and a good angel had not led a lonely wayfarer across her tracks!

But now off with my woollen cloak and I wrapped the child up as well as I could. And then it was a long distance to carry her: how I found the strength, I do not understand to this day. But I knew roughly where we were and fairly soon I found the road again. It was as if suddenly I had become another person. Never since have I felt myself so remarkably at one with creation. It was as if the All had opened his arms and let his strength flow into me, something which we can sometimes half apprehend, but seldom really experience.

The child in my arms slept peacefully.

"God bless you," whispered a voice inside me. "And one day maybe, when you are grown up and you get lost in the world with all its confusion, may our Lord send you his angel again to show you the right way."

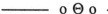

10 The mysterious rescuer

In his memoirs, Karl Sjöblom tells another story of his time spent as a schoolteacher in North Bohuslän around the turn of the century.

Deep forests, chilly lakes and mountain tops of ancient rock were the background to the life of the small and remote parish where he worked. Now a very young schoolmistress from more populated parts was employed there. She lived on the upper floor of the schoolhouse which was situated in a very isolated place. So, in those days when people had very little other transport than their own feet, she had to walk quite a long way whenever she wished to take part in any social event or even just visit friends.

One evening the young teacher was on her long trek home. Now even though for the most part the local people were friendly and rather quiet, there were nevertheless a few rowdies. Especially when they had been drinking, they became loud and quarrelsome and liable to do harm. The young teacher's heart stood still when she saw a crowd of young lads coming towards her on the road, wildly cursing and fighting.

She did not dare go on into this tumult, but what else could she do? To left and right of her was the dark forest, and in front of her the quarrelling crowd. She was in despair.

Turning her gaze to the stars, she softly murmured a prayer:

"O Father of eternal light above, look upon me in my need, send thine angel to help me."

Hardly had she spoken than a shock went through her and a mighty voice spoke:

"Follow me!"

Before her there appeared a gigantic figure — which seemed to come out of the dark space around her. The figure moved swiftly towards the oncoming crowd. Without hesitation or another thought, drawn by an invisible power, she strode calmly after the figure. And what a miracle! The fighters parted and suddenly stood silently on either side of the road. They seemed neither to see nor to hear that a protecting stranger with his charge was walking through them, but no sooner was she past than the fighting and yelling recommenced.

The teacher believed, as she said later, that she had passed through the wicked company unseen. As in a dream she had seen the dark trunks of the fir trees gliding past, for she had difficulty in keeping up with the long steps of her rescuer, and all the while she felt no fear. On and on led the giant figure and she continued to follow. It was springtime and on the lake there was still ice, but it was breaking up and there were open patches of water between. In winter she could shorten her road by crossing over on the ice, but now it was dangerous. The great figure however took no notice of the danger, but calmly strode towards the ice and on to it, as if it knew exactly where the ice was bearing. And before she could believe it, she stood with the strange figure in front of the little schoolhouse where she lived.

Up till then she had only seen the back of the stranger, but now he turned round and with a short greeting he bade her farewell. Only when she was sitting in her room and had lit the lamp did she begin to think about her strange experience. Who was this figure? A man who by chance happened to come along? Or was it a being from a higher world? Whatever or whoever it was, the mysterious figure had appeared to her in answer to her prayer and had become her rescuing angel.

When she went down to the lake the next morning the ice had completely broken up. It seemed to her a miracle that, only the night before, she had been able to cross over on it.

11 Pure coincidence?

My good friend and colleague, understandably enough in the light of what follows, is unwilling to have his name in print. But this is what he told me:

As you know my wife had a dissolved marriage behind her when we married. At her first wedding the bridal pair had received some beautiful antique candlesticks and, when the couple separated, two of the candle-sticks remained hers.

In our home they were kept hidden away on a dark shelf. It was as if they could not bear the light of day. And so they remained there as the years went by.

One day I was clearing up and, with mixed feel-ings, happened across the candlesticks. With rather forced friendliness, I asked my dear wife:

"What do you think, my love, should be done with these? They really have no use here."

The woman in my life gave no clear answer.

"Sell them?" I suggested.

"No, that would not be right."

"Give them away?"

"But to whom?"

"They haven't brought any more luck."

After some thought, we agreed that they could be exchanged for something else in the antique shop where they were bought originally. But time went by, and the candlesticks remained tucked away in their dark corner. Then I had to look for something else on the shelf, and this time I said decisively:

"Tomorrow I shall take your candlesticks into town with me!"

But when tomorrow came the weather was so bad that I put the matter off. Again a week or so passed, then I had an errand so that it suited me to take the fatal candlesticks. But unbelievably — I forgot them! I can imagine that Freud would have nodded wisely.

At last one day I was on the way with the candlesticks safely in my bag. When I left the suburban railway, I saw an acquaintance with whom I should normally have stopped to chat. But my errand caused me to turn my head the other way and go straight past him. The same happened with another person a little further down the street. I deliberately avoided them both.

At last I stood in the shop where the candlesticks had been bought many years before. No other customers, only a friendly lady behind the counter.

Was the owner (whom I knew) in? No, sorry, he had just gone out.

Rather hesitantly I explained why I had come, that I had a couple of candlesticks that I wanted to exchange for something else.

"I'll leave them here just now in any case. Give him my greetings and say that I'll phone him," I said.

"Yes, that will be all right."

I started to take the candlesticks out of the bag. I was just handing them over the counter when at that moment the door opened. I turned my head. Who should walk in but the very man who had once been the recipient of the candlesticks as a wedding present!

There is no word to describe my embarrassment.

Caught in the act! In his eyes I stood there selling the gifts which he and she had received — she who had forsaken him for my sake.

Feeling like a whipped dog, I went out into the street. But now a sudden strong feeling rose into my consciousness: in Freudian terms, a suppressed complex, a feeling of guilt which I had not wished to admit.

Two or three times my friend was deflected from his purpose of going into town with the candlesticks; and when he finally did, he might have stopped to talk to his two acquaintances, thus avoiding the critical moment of being seen when the other man came into the shop! It can be worked out purely mathematically that the chances of such a "coincidence" are precisely nil. My friend knows full well that his experience was somehow brought about by destiny.

There are some who still believe in a hidden direction to our lives.

12 A sorry plight

She was a widow. All alone she had to look after and provide for her three children. She did not find it easy for she herself had grown up in comfort and had not learnt to turn every penny twice before spending it.

In order to earn enough, she had to work within the four walls of her flat. The only tool which she had learnt to use was the pen. She knew how to write. But her income was never very great. Mostly she seemed to live stepping from one ice-floe to the next.

Yet age and care had not robbed her face of its charm. She could still make an impression on a man, especially anyone with a taste for "playing with golden apples," which was her name for a spirited conversation, an art which she herself had fully mastered.

And so destiny provided that a man did appear on the horizon. He approached her discreetly, very much the gentleman, and clearly with honourable intentions. He offered her considerable help: the relief of an almost oppressive burden. And furthermore, perhaps he could become a fatherly friend to her children. Added to which she was not averse to his charm.

One day he wrote inviting her to visit him. She realized that with this visit she must make the final decision whether to accept him or not. She was not sure. Would she be fleeing from her real destiny, or would she on the way to a new life-task? Could she trust herself to her own feelings? These and similar questions were still going through her mind as she sat in the train on her way to meet him.

The answer to these questions she received when she got off the train. She tripped as she was descending the steps and fell heavily on to the platform, where she lay with a twisted ankle and in great pain. In this helpless situation, the she certainly did not look her best. Playing with golden apples was far from her thoughts. She was treated by a doctor, laid up in bed and lay there like a wreck stranded on a foreign shore.

How she met and finally took leave of the man she never told.

"But it was a sorry plight," she said many years later with a wry grin. But then she became serious. "How much more difficult my life would have become if destiny had not taken a hand! The poor man later completely lost his way in life. He joined a religious sect and surrendered his identity completely."

13 Where was the angel?

What is "chance"? This question comes back again and again in our lives. We seize upon the word "chance" whenever we cannot find the connection between one happening and another. Understood in this way, the expression has a purely negative meaning. If the sun shines on the roof of a house and melts the ice so much that a sheet slides off, that is a sequence of cause and effect. To speak of chance in that connection is pure nonsense. If a man is walking about in the town on his business, that too arises from a sequence of events; but the two sequences have quite different original causes. Coincidence takes place when the two sequences cross each other. So in this case the man might easily have been right under the ice when it fell and he would have been killed on the spot, but he "chanced" to stop and so escaped. The crossing-point of the sequences was moved.

At this juncture, we may ask whether there is a force or being which can move the crossing-points or, so to speak, control the coincidence. Indeed anyone who has had a "lucky escape" may ask: "Was it my angel that guided events?"

Now it does not always happen that we avoid the falling ice, or whatever the danger may be. Where, then, was the angel when we were overtaken by misfortune? Absent? Taken up with something else?

Yes, where was the angel? That became an

oppressive question for two young parents. This is what they told me:

Our eldest child was four years old and already a very enterprising little fellow. It so happened then that his grandmother died. We tried as best we could to explain to him what had taken place. Time passed and it was Advent and a mild winter. One evening we were out of doors together looking up at the stars with wonder. Suddenly the child said:

"That's where Grandmother is now!" Then, after a short silence came the emphatic outburst:

"I cannot die, me!"

That was an unforgettable moment for me, his father.

After Christmas it turned cold. The river at the bottom of the valley became covered with ice, and snow came. Now the little chap wanted to go out.

"But don't go too far away from the yard," I warned him, for the boy had two slightly older friends who wanted to take him with them. "Only as far as the cross-roads, no further."

No, no, he would not go any further.

I went off to the office and was there until midday. Then the telephone rang. A neighbour was saying that our little boy had fallen into the water ... Into the water? I could not understand how that could be, but I rushed off. And there already at the crossroads stood the ambulance and police. A terrible premonition overcame me, because that road led straight down to the iced-covered river, and right out in the middle was an open stretch of water.

The two friends were crying as they told how they had gone down with the little boy to the crossroads.

44

There they had sat for a while. Then a nice dog came and they had patted it. The dog ran down further and on to the ice, and they had followed it. There they had spotted the open stretch of water and had begun to throw bits of ice into it. But it was slippery there. The smallest one slipped and fell in. He was caught by the current and dragged under, and so he was lost.

"I saw Jesus above his head," said one of the boys.

The ice was broken through and the lifeless body found. A short stay on earth was over.

"I cannot die, me!" An echo of those words still sounds in the parents' minds after all these years. From the viewpoint of earthly life a meaningless misfortune. But perhaps not from the angels' vantage point.

14 Off the pier

One cold grey Monday morning in February, my friend, the shipping agent, stood at the window of his office looking out over the wide square towards the harbour. Hardly anyone was to be seen in the street; it was still early and the usual busy traffic had not yet begun.

On the pier there were a few cars parked. Suddenly he noticed that one of the cars started to move — and rolled right off the edge of the pier. No other living soul was around on that early Monday morning; not a soul outside had noticed the catastrophe.

With a shout my friend rushed downstairs, across the square and out to the pier. Among the ice–floes he caught sight of the bulge of a green anorak. On the way he had snatched a boathook from the shed, and now he managed to hook it into the collar of the man floating among the ice. It was heavy work keeping his head up out of water. Fortunately another car came at that moment; my friend signalled to the driver and he came to help. The two of them struggled hard to keep the man up.

At last a police–car came on the scene, summoned by telephone from the agent's office. With the help of the policemen, they managed with great effort to get the unfortunate man out of the water. Now they had to act quickly to get all the water out of him.

"Get him straight to the hospital," said my friend.

As the shock of the event overcame him, he needed

a good while before he could explain to the police what had happened.

When the casualty arrived at the hospital he was "clinically dead," as they say, but the doctors managed to bring him back to life. His family in Sweden was notified.

Some weeks later he was discharged. After a long convalescence he sent a letter of thanks in which he wrote:

"Now I am as well as can be expected after what happened. But I am a completely new man, in terms of my entire life-style; my family say they do not recognize me any more. I hope that we meet again sometime."

Perhaps the event had a deeper meaning.

15 A strange warning

In his day, Professor Otto Petterson was a pioneer researcher in oceanography, and one who had the honour to be present at the opening of Alfred Nobel's will. As a young student in Uppsala he had a friend called Eisen who also became a professor. Professor Eisen was an archaeologist and had emigrated to America. For a long time they lost contact with each other and only when they were older and retired did a lively correspondence begin.

In one of his letters, Professor Eisen told of a strange experience from his student days. Late one evening he came home to his lodging. He was completely sober, for as far as he could remember he had not touched any alcohol that evening. To continue in his own words:

Suspecting nothing, I opened the door of my room and there, God preserve me, I saw myself lying on the bed. That I was startled is a mild way of putting it. Immediately I shut the door and remained standing outside. No, I must be seeing things. Gently I eased the door open a crack and peeped in. There I saw myself still lying on my back, motionless as if dead. I managed to shut the door again and ran out into the street. Not far away lived a friend and I knocked at his door. Somewhat sleepily he opened up. I stammered some excuse which I had invented on the way, and was allowed to spend the night there on a divan. But I got no sleep that night.

Next morning with the sun shining in through the window, my friend awake and his landlady bringing in the coffee, my courage and cheerfulness returned. I began to laugh out loud.

"I dare say you will want to ask what was the matter with me last night when I came rushing along half crazy," I said.

Oh, yes, he would like to know. Then I told him what I had seen through the crack in the door.

After some humorous comments, we decided to go and see whether I was still lying in the bed with my nose in the air. But when we opened the door, our laughter died. At the foot of the bed there had stood a tall tiled stove which we call a Swedish stove. In the night it had fallen down and completely crushed the bed.

16 The unconventional lodger

Shortly before the outbreak of the First World War, Rudolf Steiner's Goetheanum (at first called the "Johannesbau") was being built in Dornach near Basel. People came from many countries to help with that immense work, among them Daniel Mutach, then in his mid–thirties.

First Daniel had to find somewhere to stay and he did not know the town very well. Not far from the building–site, a short way down the hill, he came to a fine house. There he rang the bell. The lady of the house opened the door. He asked her if she had a room to let. Although she had not been thinking of letting, it so happened that she did have a room which could be let, but first she needed to put it in order. If he would come back in an hour's time, he could see it.

"No, don't worry about that, I'll just see it as it is," said Mutach, who needed the room urgently.

And to the housewife's no little astonishment, he charged up the stairs. Such an unconventional lodger she could do without, she thought. Rather reluctantly she followed him to see what he was up to. He had already thrust open the door of the room where her little daughter lay in her cot — blue in the face, almost suffocated. Mutach immediately lifted her up by her legs and a button fell out of her throat.

The mother arrived close behind. They stood without a word looking into each other's eyes.

Well, of course he did get the room!

"What was it that, against all good manners, made me run up the stairs and open the right door?" asked Daniel Mutach, when many years later, in the presence of the lady of the house, he told me the story.

17 Unbelievable

Unbelievable, yes, but true. So unbelievable that it could hardly be fiction, for what is told in fiction has to have some verisimilitude, and so fiction cannot be beyond all bounds of likelihood.

I must invoke such arguments to defend the truth of the story told by my friend and colleague — a teacher at a Swedish Steiner school — about a bizarre experience of his uncle's.

On a pleasant warm summer's day, the uncle was sitting in his room. He is a very sober gentleman, not usually given to showing his feelings. But on that day he suddenly allowed his newspaper to fall, got up from his deep armchair and went to the open window. There he did something he never usually did. With a deep breath and "Oh, how lovely!" he stretched his arms out of the window.

So far one can believe the story. But what is completely unbelievable is that at that moment, a little child fell into his arms! It must have fallen out of the window from the floor above.

My friend assured me that his good uncle was a man who had nothing to do with tall stories of any kind.

18 "Deine Emma"

Looking back on life, we can often see a point at which life took a completely new direction. These critical moments in time may be brought about by a unforeseen stroke of fate or some other quite incomprehensible event.

My grandmother, Nathalie Munch, has a story about an event of this sort. In their youth, way back in the last century, she and her brothers and sisters spent many happy years in Rome where her father was doing research in the Vatican archives. The Munch family was at that time friendly with an elderly German gentleman who had settled in Rome, a cultivated and genial person. His name was Masstaler; he was unmarried and apparently well off.

One day — this was before there were telephones — Frøken Nathalie was sent to convey an invitation to Masstaler. She found him busy sorting out some things. He had just pulled out a drawer and in his hand he was holding a beautifully crocheted silk bag, of the long narrow kind that was used to keep silver and gold coins in. Nathalie admired the beautiful work and asked if she might borrow the purse so as to crochet a copy. Without replying, Masstaler pushed the purse rather abruptly back into the drawer. But then he recollected himself and, slightly embarrassed, he took out the purse again and said something to the effect that, as she thought it was so beautiful, she could have it.

When after a while Nathalie had finished her purse,

she came to return the loan. Masstaler received her with his usual friendliness. She thanked him politely and then with a little mischievous smile she added:

"Look what I found in the purse: this gold ring with the engraving: *Deine Emma.*"

Masstaler stood there thunderstruck. Turning pale, he seized the back of a chair to steady himself.

"What are you saying?" he stammered. *"Deine* ...? You must excuse me, Frøken Munch ... I am not feeling well. I'm afraid I'll have to ask you to leave ... No, no, I don't need a doctor."

Completely taken aback, Nathalie withdrew. Some days went by. Then came a courteous letter from Masstaler asking her to pay him a visit: he had something which he wished to tell her. The elderly gentleman received her calmly and courteously as usual. Then he said that he would explain why the ring had had such a devastating effect on him.

As a young man without any means whatever, he had begun his career in a big mercantile firm in Hamburg.

"Conditions at that time were very patriarchal," he explained. "When our master had a message for his wife, he usually sent the junior in the office, and that was me. And a few times each year all the staff were invited to the family home. In this way I became acquainted with his daughter, Emma, of course at a distance. Even so there grew in me a delicious but hopeless longing. Every time I was sent up to the big house, my heart would beat faster, and each time I wondered excitedly whether I would be able to see her and exchange a few words with her. But even to think of asking for her hand? No, that was like courting the Princess of Babylon.

"The longing in my heart was almost unbearable. I whispered her name in the dark, I confided in the stars of the night. Well, to cut a long story short, in the end I imagined that I saw something in her eyes which might be taken as affection. That nourished my delicious agony till in the end I plucked up desperate courage, sat down and wrote a long letter in which I confided to her my heart's secret. My prospects were anything but great, I wrote, I had nothing to offer except my invincible love. But it had happened before in the history of the world that two hearts despite all obstacles had been able to be united ...

"Then I sent off the letter. In a fever I waited for an answer. But no answer came. Finally, after two unendurable weeks, I was sent an empty purse, without any accompanying word.

"It was the worst moment of my life, for it could only mean rejection, along with a mocking indication of my poverty. That's what I thought at the time. And so I swore an oath that the purse should be filled, but never laid at her feet."

The old man continued with difficulty:

"The worst now is to imagine what Emma must have believed, that I had only made a fool of her. She has long since passed over the threshold to a better world."

He paused for a moment, then he uttered calmly:

"It was not to be. A higher power held its hands before my eyes."

The ring engraved *"Deine Emma"* he presented to my grandmother.

19 Shipwreck on the Rundskalle

In the skerries off Bohuslän on the west coast of Sweden, there is an island called the Rundskalle (the Round Skull). The island got its name because from a distance it resembles a huge skull sticking up out of the sea. Right down at the shore stands a house, low and old. Nowadays it is only used as a holiday house in summer.

In former times on the Rundskalle there lived a fisher–family, man and wife with a large flock of children. And then something so remarkable happened there one Christmas Eve that it has not been forgotten to this day.

During the forenoon of Christmas Eve — that is on the Day of Adam and Eve — the father had been away on business over in the town on the mainland. When he was sailing back home, he had the wind against him and the sky hung low over the sea. There was something in the air which he knew only too well — as if Our Lord's clenched fist were hidden behind the clouds. But he knew every reef and skerry so he had no difficulty in making his way.

By the time he had come in under the lee of the Rundskalle, the wind had risen to a stiff breeze. In safety he moored his boat, came ashore and soon he was with his family getting everything ready for the festival. Meanwhile the weather had worsened.

"God be merciful to those at sea tonight," said the wife.

The storm-wind was driving the high spring tide up the shore and the sea was washing right up to the walls of the house. Even so perhaps the worst was not the wind but the beginning of a snowstorm.

In bad weather the people on the Rundskalle would light a light on top of the island where there was a cresset for that purpose. But that evening it would not be much good. The snowstorm would blot out the signal a few ship's lengths away. All the same the father told his eldest son to go up on to the hill with the light.

Apart from that not much was said. At last they were all sitting round the laid table and in front of each one was burning a home-made candle, while outside the storm raged round the roof and walls and the sea crashed upon the rocks. It was sea and storm that rang in the festival for the family on the Rundskalle that Christmas Eve.

In front of the father the Bible lay open. He had just been reading the Gospel about the shepherds in the fields, and all were sitting with folded hands for now he was about to read the prayers.

Then it happened. With a crash that could have heralded the end of the world, the bowsprit of a large ship came in through the window. Bits of glass came flying over the table and the floor. The candles and the lamp were blown out and sea-spray came flying in. Immediately the room was turned into a confusion of upset chairs and shocked people.

Only the father realized at once what had happened. Out into the storm he went with his eldest sons carrying lights, ropes and boat-hooks. Shouts and broken commands could be heard amid the storm and darkness. The ship heeled over and, under the force of

57

the wind, started to break up, the keel cracking and timbers splintering.

A line came flying, thrown at random by someone on board. One of the boys managed to get hold of it and the hawser followed. Those on shore hauled away until they could make the hawser fast and so bring the crew to shore before the ship was pounded to bits. The helmsman was lashed fast and he had to be cut loose.

The ship was English, and no one on the Rundskalle could speak that language. Nor could the ship's crew speak Swedish. But one language they could all understand: *thankfulness*.

They all helped each other to patch up as well as they could the hole which the bowsprit had made. And then they celebrated together, there in the cottage on the Rundskalle, a Christmas Eve like no other before or since. Once more the old saying was proved true: where there is room in the heart there is room in the house. And food was found for everyone, and that in itself was half a miracle, said the mother when she told later what had happened.

While the sea and the storm raged outside, Swedish and English psalms were sung in that lowly fisherman's cottage. But high up behind the clouds, the mighty fist had unclenched: God's hands were spread in blessing over the earth.

20 God's loan

Looking back on our childhood, we can sometimes recall a face or a word which in a strange way has a deeper echo in our memory, almost as if the person who said the word was overshadowed for a moment by a higher being, something much greater than himself, but without realizing it.

I was nine years old when it was my good fortune to stay with Jorun one summer at Tordhol. Jorun was for the most part quiet and serious; but a nicer person I have never met, nor seen bluer eyes.

Everything was done in the old-fashioned ways on the farm at that time, and Jorun was busy all day long. Even I now was just grown-up enough to realize that life could not consist only of play and useless games. No, it was something quite different to be with Jorun and to help in the byre and the farmhouse.

As it was now summer, most of the cattle were up on the high pastures. But the byre was not quite empty, for there were still a few home-cows, which on being called home in the evening would come lumbering down from the hills, round and well-fed. And Jorun could call them better than anyone else. First she would call:

"Cow, my poor wee one, come now, come now!" Then her call would rise on a surging wave of notes to an incredible pitch, rising and falling, rising and falling again ... This way of calling cattle is known as *hulle*. You could really believe that she had learnt it inside the mountains — from a fairy.

And the cows would answer with a long moo:
"We are coming now."

It so happened that one of the home-cows calved
and was kept in for a day or two. And now the new-
born calf was to have a good drink: an *einlåg* mixed
with meal. The *einlåg* was a brew of fresh juniper and
in former times was much used for internal as well as
external cleansing. Over the hearth in the far corner of
the byre stood a large iron cauldron in which the
juniper was to be brewed. Jorun took some straw to
rub down the calf which had just stood up.

"Perhaps you can get the fire going under the pot,"
said she to me.

Oh yes, there lay the wood handy. But for some
reason or other, the fire would not light as it should.
Perhaps the wood was a bit green. I fanned it, but that
did not help much. Then I took some dry hay and laid
it on the embers. Jorun caught sight of this.

Unforgettable, so gentle and earnest was she when
she took my head between her hands and looked into
my face.

"Thou must not do that, laddie," she said in her
dialect. "Thou must mind that hay is bread for cattle,
and bread, bread is *Gudslån* (God's loan)!"

Her face had the aura of an angel.

At that time I did not understand what Jorun meant
by *Gudslån*. But I had something to think about, and
life has since taught me to understand.

22 Hardly an angel?

He looked like a descendant of the Thrall Kark who killed Jarl Håkon in the old saga of Olav Tryggvason. And he was no angel, poor fellow. So perhaps he does not really belong in this series. We never heard him called anything else but "Skålhanan." His children were thin and grey and we did not play with them.

They lived in a poor cottage a little bit off the highway. People laughed when they told how his wife beat him every Saturday night because he often took a drop too many. The way she used her tongue, she was quite capable of that.

"Carry the fellow home and put him on bags of gold and silver, lads," she would call after us who were so to speak children of richer folk.

When Skålhanan came along the road, we ran and hid behind the wall.

"Skålhanan! Skålhanan!" we shouted when he came unsteadily along for it often happened that he was reeling quite a bit, but never once did he turn his yellow face towards us.

One day I came across Skålhanan sitting in our kitchen. He was shy and small and sat on the edge of his chair as if he did not want to make it any dirtier than he could help. He had come to speak to my father about some work in the harbour. I remember the rank smell of his clothes.

Years went by. We had long since moved to other parts of the country. I had grown up and Skålhanan never entered my thoughts any more. Then it so happened that I went back to the scene of my child-hood. I saw again the places that I had not seen since I was eight years old. There was the old quarry with the dam where my brother and I used to sail over to England, and there was the well that never had any water in it. There we had played, and there ... much had gone and much had changed.

I wandered up to the woods above the house which had once been our childhood home and I suddenly came upon a little clearing — something which had once been a patch of field, a narrow strip surrounded by big boulders. The scent of flowers and hay was so good. How lovely I thought — ox-eye daisies in their Sunday best, bluebells and smiling buttercups. But what hard work it must have been — then it suddenly struck me: was not this where Skålhanan lived? Yes, of course, there indeed stood the poor little cottage all tumbledown, grey and forsaken, there the empty woodsheds.

The people had left. Skålhanan, whom we had mocked, his wife who used to beat him ... I stayed a long time beside the ruined fence. No indeed, neither he nor his wife was what you would call an angel. But how beautiful it was there after they had gone. It was as if the flowers were giving thanks for a life lived in humble poverty.

I had to ask myself: what shall we leave in our place once we have gone?

23 Mother Inez

At home my father had become ill. The doctor had ordered complete peace and quiet in the house for a period, and so I was sent to Mother Inez. She lived a long way away from us by the Swedish border where her husband was a customs official. The house stood in a lonely place surrounded by endless forests. It was full of children, big and little. Being with Mother Inez was like being where the sun always shines. When she smiled, which she did quietly and calmly, her eyes sparkled with light, and her hair stood like a shining glory round her head. It was as if an angel lived in her. Who knows?

Mother Inez was Swedish, and all her days she spoke with a Swedish lilt. We children thought that was so beautiful.

I was not the first to be a guest of Inez and kind Søren, her husband. The children often spoke about Same-Lars and so I became curious and Inez had to tell me about him.

It was late one winter's evening about Christmas time, she began, dark outside and snow falling thickly. The youngest children were already in bed, and the bigger ones were just about to go to bed. There was a knock on the outer door. Half-scared they listened. The main highway to Sweden passed close by and it could be a tramp or vagabond. But at that time of the year and with night falling? Not many would knock at that time. There was no second knock.

"You had better go and see who it is, Søren," said Inez.

He opened the door. Outside on the doorstep lay a figure collapsed in a heap. It was a young woman. Søren helped her in, and then they saw that it was a Lapp-girl. She had been dismissed from service on one of the big farms lower down in the village because she was pregnant.

Inez came with a light in her hands.

"Heavens above," she exclaimed.

The girl had waded through mud and snow up to her knees. Now she was at the end of her strength and shivering with cold. The children at first gathered round and stared, but then they had to keep out of the way. The first thing was to get the stove going and put milk on to warm. Then to get the girl to bed.

A few days later she gave birth to her baby, a little boy who was given the name Lars. Mother Inez was the midwife and later took charge of what was to be done, for the Lapp girl had no idea. The young father of the child had left her in the lurch and at first did not want to accept any responsibility. But Inez was adamant! Her standing in the parish for morality was so good that the man did not succeed in avoiding his paternal obligation.

The little mother was herself little more than a child.

"Stay with us till the baby is weaned and does not need its mother's milk any more. Then you can go back to your family in the Jämtland Mountains," advised Inez to comfort her. "Cheer up and remember that a child always brings great blessing!"

Hearing such words, the young mother brightened up.

But little Lapp Lars could not stay permanently with Inez and Søren for there were already ten children in the house; Inez had to find a good home for him. How that came about is a story in itself, for in the children's home where the little one was to go, Inez discovered things were not at all as they should be. All that had to be cleared up first. Without hesitation, Inez took on the unpleasant duty of stirring up the authorities to put the matter right.

Ten children — how did that come about? Inez had been a teacher in the south of Sweden. She had been young, beautiful and vivacious, and you can imagine that she was much sought after. There appeared on the scene a very "fine gentleman," a widower. He flat-tered her. He bought her expensive gifts, silk dresses and jewellery. She was invited to accompany him to the theatre and to concerts, and to mix in good society. He even asked her to go to London with him. Inez did not really know how she should respond to such magnificent offers.

Then something frightful happened. The fine gentleman was suddenly arrested. It turned out that he had committed terrible crimes. He had poisoned his two former wives to get huge insurances. In prison he committed suicide.

Inez could not stay in the town any longer. She had to go far away from everything and from all those who knew about the scandal. Away up in Härjedalen by the Norwegian frontier, she took a job as a teacher. And now she was as much alone as before she had been in company.

One day in winter she put on her skis and took a run over the pass into Norway. At the customs post there she made good friends, a young couple, Søren and his wife with four children.

After that there were frequent ski journeys back and forth over the border. Together they baked bread, sang and had many happy times. Inez helped with the children. She and Søren's wife grew very fond of each other. In due course, the wife was going to have another baby. Often she was unwell and had to rest, then Inez would stay and comb her friend's long and lovely hair. Latterly her friend's condition grew worse.

Then one night back at home, Inez had a dream. She dreamed she was in her friend's house who was lying pale in bed with her masses of hair all undone. Her friend took from under her night-dress a new-born child, held it out to Inez and said:

"Now you must look after this."

At that moment Inez woke up. She felt that something must have happened. She looked at the clock; it was half past two. She got no more sleep that night.

Next day she cut her lessons short, and went off to see what had happened. Oh yes, the child had been born and was alive, but the mother was dead — she died at half past two in the morning. In the house there was weeping and despair.

That was a hard time for Inez. Back and forth she went over the mountain, almost six miles each way. Then the thaw set in and she could not get through. That summer, Søren and the children were moved to another frontier post further north in Trøndelag.

Time went by. Now a new gentleman began to have his eye on Inez: the priest in the town. He was a bachelor, and it was rumoured that he was well off. He was so nice to Inez, always coming and paying his respects to her.

Then there came a letter from Søren, a cry in desperation. He was completely at his wits' end. For help he had only a half-witted girl, for the frontier post was so lonely that no one else would serve in his house. Could Inez come? There were still some weeks of the summer holidays left. Inez set off on the mountain road.

The sight which met her was terrible: the children filthy, unkempt and crawling with lice; no decent chairs or table in the house, only a few boxes nailed together to sit on; dirt and filth everywhere. And Søren sunk in despair. Years later, Inez confessed that at that moment she had gone outside and wept.

"But," I then said to myself, "lice don't like water."

Fortunately the weather was good and so she gathered together the children:

"We're all going to move to the barn for a week! All the bedding and clothes we shall put in the river with stones to hold them down, and they will stay there till every blessed louse is drowned ..."

There followed a great washing and cleaning for days on end; darning and patching, mending furniture and putting everything to rights. And it was unbelievable how snug they made everything with the simplest means, stools made of nothing but tree-roots and much else besides. After two weeks, the whole house smelled of green soap and fresh juniper. The children shone like new minted shillings, and the youngest ones had already begun to call her mother. When the time came for Inez to go away, there they stood, their sadness reflected in their faces, for they could not really understand why.

It was term time again. The priest came regularly

and listened to her teaching. He was greatly interested. And then he told how he often sat so alone at home in the evenings; could Inez not come and visit him sometimes? The vicarage door stood open; she knew the way, did she not?

But Inez had also seen something in Søren's eyes when they had said good-bye. She did not dare think about it — a man with hardly a penny and a heap of lousy children. Well, she did not have to wait long before another letter came, a letter asking her to marry him.

Meantime the priest came again to listen to her teaching and praised it. That was pleasant. Yes, and would she consider moving after a while.

What did he mean? She was happy enough with her position.

"No, not away from the town. Only down to the vicarage!"

So Inez was being pulled from two sides. She could not answer yes or no. Neither to the priest nor to Søren either.

"I asked for help from him who knows more than we human beings," she said. "And help I received, but it was against my own will and wishes. I had a dream which I could not ignore. In the dream I walked by a lake. There came two fishes swimming to the shore. One was fat and shining, and the other was thin. I dreamed that I took them up out of the water and opened them. In the first one I found nothing, but in the other there lay a large shining pearl.

"The next day I wrote to Søren and you can guess what I wrote. But I cannot say that I wrote with a light heart. Oh, what a fool I was!"

Here Inez laughed, though I saw that she had tears

in her eyes and that she had to take out her hand-kerchief.

"But oh, we were so poor," she went on, "especi-ally at the beginning. Sometimes we did not know where to find the next meal. Bread without butter, potatoes, but no herring. But never for a moment did I regret it. I told the children stories instead of some-thing to put on their bread, so that they forgot how harsh our fare was. And Søren and I were so happy. He was so good-hearted. But we had to make shift for every penny. Never shall I forget the day when Søren came home bringing a cow. Just imagine, our own cow! You should have seen the children, they hopped and danced, they stroked and patted it. Then off they went to get grass for it. I think that was the greatest festival day in my life for now we were over the worst."

That was how Inez told me the story the last time I saw her. She had grown old and white-haired but with the same glory round her head. She told me, and I could understand, that she knew she had been supported by the hand of an invisible helper through-out her life.

24 The image and form of angels

Pictures of God are human creations. The same can be said of our pictures of angels. But behind the human face we sense the countenance of the Creator. From olden times that has been a natural conception with nearly all cultures, though not with the Jews of the Old Testament which tells us that even Moses was not able to see his God face to face: "but you cannot see my face; for man shall not see me and live" (Ex.33:20). Only from *behind* could Moses see the Lord.

For that chosen people, therefore, the law was established that they should not make any image of their spiritual supersensible living God. All this changed when God's Son became man in the Messiah. As man he had become sensibly present among men, and thus God's countenance had become the human countenance.

From this point on, the door was opened for Christian art. In faith, the artist could ascend to a vision of Christ's face and could represent it freely as it appeared to him. Christian art could then also present angels. They were depicted as most beautiful winged beings, messengers of the Godhead. Winged, in order to indicate that as spiritual supersensible beings, they were not subject to gravity. Higher orders of angels appeared even with two or three pairs of wings.

This then has been our traditional picture, one

which was corrected for my friend Oddbjørn Birke-
land by a unique encounter. Here is his account.

*I had the job of teaching immigrants, refugees from
distant countries seeking asylum with us in Norway.
Above all they had to learn our language, but also to
gain some insight into our customs and practices.*

*When Advent came we were discussing the ap-
proaching festival of Christmas and how it was
celebrated in our country. We practised a Christmas
carol with the line: "Angels from the realms of
glory."*

"Angels, what are angels?" I was asked.

*How was I to explain? I seized some chalk and
tried to draw one, with scant success. With a few
sketchy lines, I indicated the wings.*

*In the break after the lesson, I was approached by
a man about thirty-five years old from South America. Quietly and confidentially he told me:*

*"Angels do not really look like that. An angel is
more like a kernel of light surrounded by a gentle
glow."*

*He showed me what he meant with a little sketch.
When I asked him whether he had himself experienced
one, he told me his story.*

*He had been put under torture in his own country,
more or less psychologically for some months, and
then physically for three days. At the end of the third
day, he had been stretched out on a table and felt that
he could not bear any more. Then he went out of his
physical body and experienced a wonderful lightness
and freedom. He passed first through a kind of room
and came into something like a tunnel through which
he travelled at great speed. Far a way he saw a great*

light which he felt was waiting for him, and which he felt he should go towards, because he had a connection with it. It was then that he saw the angels. They accompanied him on both sides — each as he had described them but with different colour–tones of light, each according to his "order" as he thought. He felt that he was moving away from the earth and that the angels were trying to hold him back. Only when he had come quite near to the great light did the angels succeed in stopping him. And the light spoke to him:

"Not yet is it time for you!"

In order to help him, I corrected his Norwegian slightly at this point, but he insisted and said, no, it was exactly as he had heard it. He had been sent back, so to speak, followed by the angels. On the way back, he was fully aware that he had to pass through one or two different worlds or conditions before he could enter his physical body again. And the last was truly "terrible," as he expressed it.

This man's account bears an unmistakable resemblance to the near–death experiences of those pronounced "clinically dead." Such accounts have been known and published for some years.

25 Talking with angels

Is it possible to talk to an angel? Many will shake their heads. Or if asked whether they had ever tried, they would probably reject the very suggestion with an indulgent smile. Those few, however, who have seriously tried will keep silent, for the most part. One does not speak readily and openly about such intimate experiences.

Of course what we usually understand by "conversation" must here take on a different meaning. Do the angels listen to our questions? Often our questions seem to go unanswered. Why? Perhaps because we ask about things that do not require an answer from the angels, or perhaps simply because we are not capable of hearing the answers. It may even be that those who put the questions cannot really find the words to express what has been communicated to them.

Angels do listen to questions put with earnestness and sincerity. Rudolf Steiner advised that we should present a question to the world of the angels before we go to sleep, and when we wake up, we may find the answer in the depths of our own soul.

At times especially when some spiritually productive work will not go forward, a conversation with the angel can work wonders. Anyone who is involved in writing, or in any similarly creative spiritual work, can from time to time end up in a dead-end. The work becomes stuck, inspiration dries up or one's mind fills with things that clearly do not come from "above."

Those who turn in their need towards a higher help-giving power will seldom be turned away empty-handed.

But if faith is lacking? Here we must realize that faith does not always mean holding fast to one's favourite ideas, but means rather an inward openness, a trusting approach.

In this mood, not particularly thinking of angels, a young man was going along a lonely road one winter's evening. He had left behind him his day's work, and he breathed in the peace of nature. In the shadow of a high mountain, he sat down upon a stone. In front of him, stars were reflected in a little lake. Not a breath of wind was to be felt.

He sat in contemplation as the moon slowly rose from behind the dark mountain. This moon seemed to him to be familiar in a remarkable way.

"Are you not the door, through which I came into my life upon earth?" he asked, "and should I not remember?"

Then suddenly it seemed to him that memories rose within him: a weaving dance of souls approaching the earth, and he amidst them; but the memories were filled with a power and intensity that can hardly be described.

Now he was sitting there in his poor earth-reality, and he seemed utterly small and weak in comparison with the power of that existence before birth.

The memory sank down within him nor did it ever come back to be experienced again. But a great question remained within him: is it higher beings who infuse with their might and power those souls that are not yet born?

26 Conclusion

If one embarks upon a study of Rudolf Steiner's spiritual science, otherwise known as anthroposophy, one learns of an abundance of different spirit and soul beings, among them the angels. It must be said, however, that for many people today the study of anthroposophy can present a formidable undertaking, even for so-called believers.

For modern theology, on the other hand, the question of whether or not angels exist has become a very minor one, and their intervention in the destiny of the soul is hardly, if at all, touched upon. This loss of interest on the part of theology is the result of a demythologizing process whereby the older pictorial and imaginative thinking has been cast out in order to approach the truth through pure reason. But have we not cast out truth along with the pictorial and imaginative thinking? The old pictorial and imaginative world-view experienced the angelic world as a reality. "Nine are the choirs of angels" declares the old German hymn. Dionysus the Areopagite speaks of a nine-tiered sphere of angelic beings. But later critical research discredited this view: interest and belief in angels waned as agnosticism gained ground.

But just as Champollion through his work of genius has enabled us now to decipher and understand the pictorial script — the hieroglyphs — of the Ancient Egyptians, so can spiritual science not only interpret for us the pictorial and imaginative religious thinking of former ages but also enable us to approach the underlying spiritual reality of the angelic world.

Among the angelic beings, there are differences of kind, grade and rank. Different but related beings have revealed themselves in different forms to different peoples and different epochs. Thus there is a difference between the Valkyries of the Nordic peoples, the Moirai of the Greeks. the Amshaspands of the Ancient Iranians, and above all between these beings and the angels of the Old and New Testaments.

All of these beings however have intervened in the ordering of human destiny. From the earthly point of view of fortune and misfortune, this intervention does not always appear benign. Fate may appear as grim and terrible. And yet from a higher point of view, a given destiny may appear quite differently. As an illustration, here is an experience of our time. A mother who had been evacuated from Dresden with her four children during the second World War tells her story:

My husband was at the front. I myself and the children had come to live in a little country town out of harm's way. One day I sent my two eldest daughters back to the city to fetch some things from the empty ugliness. The connections were bad, so the girls had to spend the night at home in the city. That was the night when Dresden was bombed. Our daughters never returned. I myself had sent them to their deaths.

The pain in her voice had not gone away. But behind it lay a profound knowledge: she knew that her daughters were in the world of life where death is transformed into life — just as birth seen from the spiritual world can appear as death.

"I died when I was born," once said a six or seven-year old boy.

Certainly just as many stories tell of a lack of angelic help as those which tell of their rescuing care. Obviously we are inclined to imagine the higher worlds much too simply. Nowhere is it said that angels are almighty. Undoubtedly they look down upon human affairs from quite a different standpoint from that which measures life and fortune in terms of earth existence. And they have to stay within the conditions of destiny and these vary with each individual.

The difficulty today is that for a long time people have had imprinted in them much too simple ideas about life's deeper meaning. They expect everything spiritual to be so terribly simple so that even the poorest understanding can grasp it.

We all know that Nature around us is full of contradictions and is very complex. Powers and principles work against each other and fight for supremacy, but in the end they hold each other in a certain equilibrium: heat and cold, light and darkness, growth and decay, and so on. If one principle becomes absolutely dominant it works destructively, however good it is in itself. The "good" in Nature arises sometimes amid cooperation, sometimes in strife with obstacles.

To understand Nature, simple ideas do not suffice. But what about the spiritual worlds? Through a spiritual science appropriate for our times, our horizons can be widened. Our experience of fortune and misfortune in life will not be lessened. But our attitude changes; we begin to comprehend a little more deeply our existence upon earth, and our union with the spirit will become much more real. Thus we gain a stronger trust in the meaning of life and strengthened hope for a wise guidance of our destiny.

This guidance can be felt as being touched inwardly. Gradually a more conscious interaction in feeling and thinking with the world of angels arises. We can then sense that the angels draw strength from what we offer to them by way of thought and feeling. Much will depend upon this. Not that we pretend that we shall thereby become "better people," but we believe that we shall be able to fulfil our life-task better.

And that belief is a most valuable acquisition in life.